FRANK MILLER

SIN CITY

FRANK MILLER'S

THE HARD GOODBYE

SIN CITY

DARK HORSE BOOKS™

publisher
MIKE RICHARDSON

editor
RANDY STRADLEY

sin city classic logo design
STEVE MILLER

cover design
CHIP KIDD

book design
CHIP KIDD
CARY GRAZZINI
LIA RIBACCHI

FRANK MILLER'S SIN CITY® VOLUME 1: THE HARD GOODBYE

This volume collects stories originally published in issues fifty-one through sixty-two of the Dark Horse comic book series *Dark Horse Presents* and in the *Dark Horse Presents Fifth Anniversary Special*.

Published by
Dark Horse Books
A division of Dark Horse Comics, Inc.
10956 SE Main Street
Milwaukie, Oregon 97222

darkhorse.com

Second Edition: February 2005
ISBN 1-59307-293-7

1 0

PRINTED IN THE UNITED STATES OF AMERICA

FOR LYNN

SHE SMELLS
LIKE ANGELS
OUGHT TO SMELL.

11

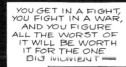

YOU GET IN A FIGHT, YOU FIGHT IN A WAR, AND YOU FIGURE ALL THE WORST OF IT WILL BE WORTH IT FOR THE ONE BIG MOMENT—

—BUT THIS...

...ONE LAST TIME I WONDER WHY...

...THEN SHE FALLS AGAINST ME...

—BUT THAT MOMENT, AS GOOD AS IT IS, IT'S NEVER GOOD ENOUGH—

...DRIPPING WITH THAT ANGEL SWEAT OF HERS...

...THE PERFECT WOMAN. THE GODDESS.

GOLDIE.

SHE SAYS HER NAME IS GOLDIE.

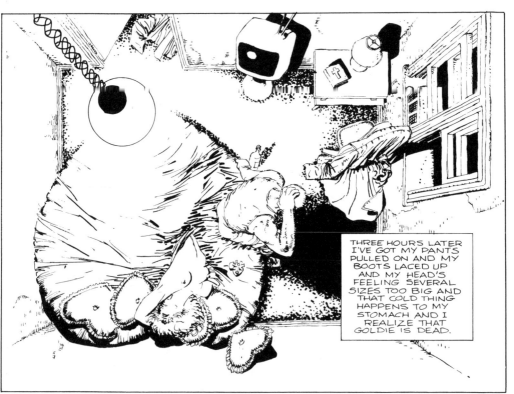

THREE HOURS LATER I'VE GOT MY PANTS PULLED ON AND MY BOOTS LACED UP AND MY HEAD'S FEELING SEVERAL SIZES TOO BIG AND THAT COLD THING HAPPENS TO MY STOMACH AND I REALIZE THAT GOLDIE IS DEAD.

NOT A MARK ON HER. YOU'D HAVE TO CHECK HER PULSE OR NOTICE THOSE PERFECT BREASTS OF HERS AREN'T MOVING LIKE THEY WOULD IF SHE WAS BREATHING.

AND THERE'S NOTHING TELLING ME IT WASN'T JUST A HEART ATTACK IN HER SLEEP...

...NOTHING BUT THAT COLD THING IN MY GUT GETTING COLDER...

...AND IT'S BEEN TOO DAMNED MANY TIMES ACROSS TOO DAMNED MANY YEARS FOR ME TO EVEN QUESTION THAT FEELING.

SHE WAS MURDERED AND I WAS RIGHT HERE WHEN IT HAPPENED, LYING NEXT TO HER, STONE DRUNK JUST LIKE SHE WAS.

DAMN IT, GOLDIE. WHO WERE YOU AND WHO WANTED YOU DEAD?

WHO WERE YOU BESIDES AN ANGEL OF MERCY GIVING A TWO-TIME LOSER LIKE ME THE NIGHT OF HIS LIFE?

GOD KNOWS WHY. IT SURE AS HELL WASN'T MY LOOKS...

...NOT MY LOOKS OR ANYTHING ELSE ABOUT ME. DAMES WITHOUT A TENTH OF WHAT YOU HAD TO OFFER WRITE ME OFF AS THE MACHO PIG I AM.

SO WHY THAT SLEAZY SALOON? WHY THAT SLOW SMILE? WHY THE KINDNESS, GOLDIE?

WHY, I ASK NOW. BUT WHEN YOU GOT SCARED, WHEN YOU TREMBLED AND YOUR EYES WENT BIG AS A LITTLE GIRL'S, I DIDN'T ASK WHY, NOT THEN.

THEN, I DIDN'T GIVE A DAMN WHAT WAS BOTHERING YOU.

ALL OF A SUDDEN SOMETHING OUTSIDE SCREAMS.

COMING THIS WAY.

COPS...THEY'RE TELLING ME TOO MUCH, SHOWING UP BEFORE ANYBODY BUT ME AND THE KILLER COULD KNOW THERE'S BEEN A MURDER.

DAMN...

NO TIME TO HIDE.

NO POINT IN PLAYING GOOD CITIZEN, EITHER. SIN CITY COPS HAVE HAD THEIR HANDS ON ME BEFORE. THIS TIME THEY WON'T MAKE THE MISTAKE OF LETTING ME LIVE.

NO REASON AT ALL TO PLAY IT QUIET.

NO REASON TO PLAY IT ANY WAY BUT MY WAY.

WHOEVER
KILLED YOU
IS GOING TO
PAY, GOLDIE...

2

WE'RE SUPPOSED TO CALL THEM *COPS*--

--BUT EVERYBODY KNOWS WHO THEY'RE WORKING FOR AND WHAT IT TAKES TO KEEP THEM HAPPY.

SOMEBODY PAID GOOD MONEY FOR THIS FRAME...

24

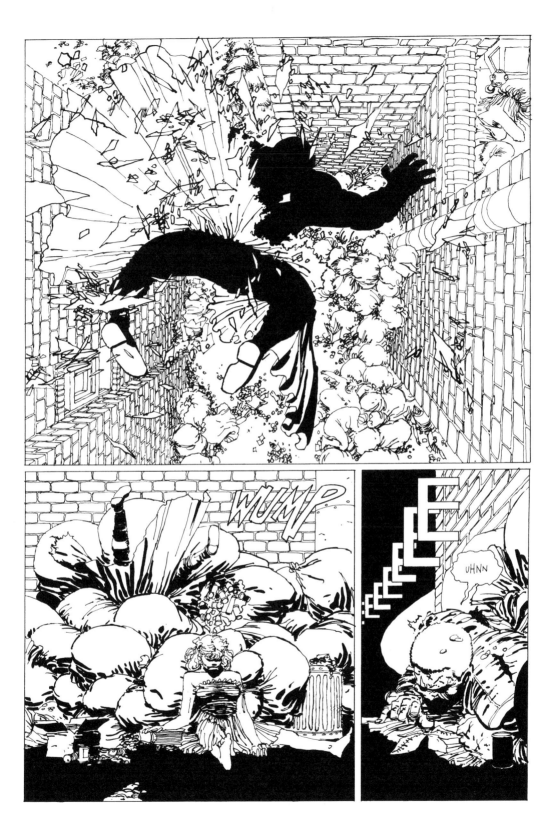

I DON'T KNOW WHY YOU DIED, GOLDIE.

I DON'T KNOW WHY AND I DON'T KNOW HOW AND HELL I NEVER EVEN MET YOU BEFORE TONIGHT BUT YOU WERE A FRIEND AND MORE WHEN I NEEDED ONE AND WHEN I FIND OUT WHO DID IT IT WON'T BE QUICK OR QUIET LIKE IT WAS WITH YOU.

NO, IT'LL BE LOUD AND NASTY, MY KIND OF KILL.

I'LL STARE THE BASTARD IN THE FACE AND LAUGH AS HE SCREAMS TO GOD AND I'LL LAUGH HARDER WHEN HE WHIMPERS LIKE A BABY.

AND WHEN HIS EYES GO DEAD THE HELL I SEND HIM TO WILL SEEM LIKE HEAVEN AFTER WHAT I'VE DONE TO HIM.

I LOVE YOU, GOLDIE.

BY NOW THERE'S TWO DOZEN COPS UP ON THE PIER, GUNS COCKED, WAITING FOR ME TO SURFACE SO THEY CAN BLAST MY FACE TO KINGDOM COME.

I HOPE THEY'RE HOLDING THEIR BREATH, THE BASTARDS...

CHIKK

KOFF

OH. IT'S
YOU.

DON'T WORRY,
LUCILLE. I
WAS JUST
GRAZED. GOT
ANY BEERS
AROUND
THIS PLACE?

LUCILLE'S MY PAROLE OFFICER. SHE'S A DYKE BUT GOD KNOWS WHY.

WITH THAT BODY OF HERS SHE COULD HAVE ANY MAN SHE WANTS.

THE PILLS COME FROM HER GIRLFRIEND WHO'S A SHRINK.

SHE TRIED TO ANALYZE ME ONCE BUT GOT TOO SCARED.

40

NOW FOR GLADYS.

SWEET GLADYS.

BUT I'LL HAVE TO SNEAK PAST MOM.

AND HER EARS HAVE GOTTEN A WHOLE LOT BETTER SINCE SHE WENT BLIND.

MOM STILL HASN'T CHANGED A THING IN THIS ROOM. EVERY WEEK SHE DUSTS IT ALL OFF SO IT LOOKS LIKE IT WAS ONLY YESTERDAY I MOVED OUT.

AND EVERY TIME I COME VISIT SHE HAS ME SLEEP IN HERE AND THE OLD SMELLS MAKE ME CRY LIKE THEY DO RIGHT NOW.

I KNEW GLADYS WOULD BE SAFE HERE.

I STOLE HER OFF THE TOUGHEST GUY I EVER MESSED WITH, BACK IN SCHOOL. HE WAS DEAD AT THE TIME SO HE DIDN'T MISS HER.

I CALL HER GLADYS AFTER ONE OF THE SISTERS FROM SCHOOL. SHE'S ALMOST LIVED UP TO THE NAME.

FOR A WHILE WE JUST GET THE FEEL OF EACH OTHER BACK, GOOD AS EVER.

I TELL HER ABOUT GOLDIE AND WHAT WE HAVE TO DO.

MARVIN? IS THAT YOU, BABY?

YES, MOM. SORRY I WOKE YOU UP.

I WAS ALWAYS GOOD AT JIGSAW PUZZLES.

BACK IN SCHOOL I HAD THIS BUDDY, NAME OF CHUCK. HE WAS RETARDED. HE'D WATCH ME PUT THE PIECES TOGETHER AND I LOVED THAT GUY BECAUSE HE WAS THE ONLY PERSON I EVER MET WHO WAS DUMB ENOUGH TO THINK I WAS A GENIUS.

AND THE SITUATION I GOT RIGHT NOW, IT'S JUST ONE MORE JIGSAW PUZZLE. PROBLEM IS I'M DAMN SHORT ON PIECES.

I'VE BEEN FRAMED FOR MURDER AND THE COPS ARE IN ON IT. BUT THE REAL ENEMY, THE SON OF A BITCH WHO KILLED THE ANGEL LYING NEXT TO ME, HE'S OUT THERE SOMEWHERE, OUT OF SIGHT, THE BIG MISSING PIECE THAT'LL GIVE ME THE HOW AND THE WHY AND A FACE AND A NAME AND A SOUL TO SEND SCREAMING INTO HELL.

THE GOOD NEWS IS THAT THE KILLER ISN'T SITTING BACK AND WAITING FOR THE COPS TO POLISH ME OFF. *"THERE WERE SOME MEN WHO CAME LOOKING FOR YOU,"* MOM SAID. *"THEY WEREN'T POLICE."*

SO ALL I GOT TO DO IS SEND THE BASTARD AN INVITATION. HE'LL COME OR HE'LL SEND SOMEBODY AND EITHER WAY IF I DON'T GET DEAD I'M BOUND TO WIND UP WITH ONE OR TWO MORE PUZZLE PIECES.

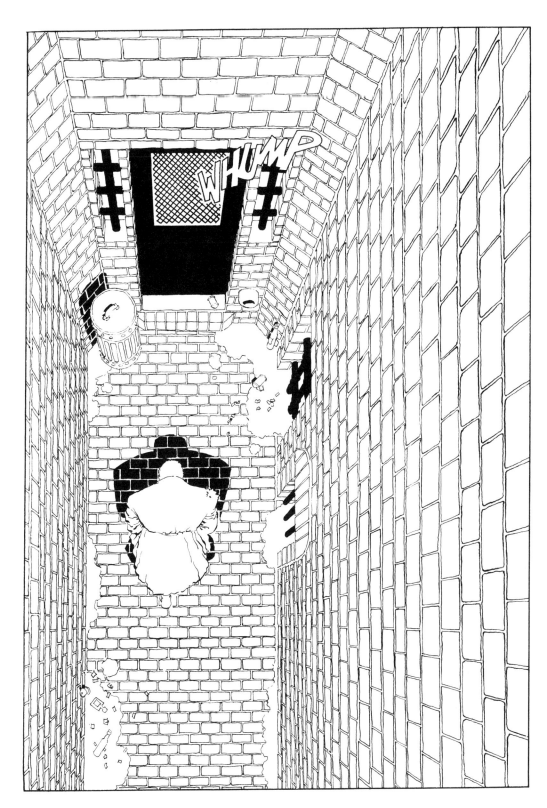

AND YOU--YOUR COAT LOOKS LIKE BAGHDAD. SO'S YOUR FACE. TAKE OFF.

TELL KADIE IT'S MARV. IT'LL BE OKAY.

OKAY.

HE'S NEW HERE, MARV. HE DIDN'T KNOW.

IN THIS TOWN JUST ABOUT ANYTHING *YOU* CAN NAME THAT'S WORTH DOING IS AGAINST THE LAW. IT WORKS OUT BETTER FOR EVERYBODY THIS WAY. COPS AND POLITICIANS MAKE THEIR FORTUNES BY LOOKING THE OTHER WAY WHILE CROOKS LIKE KADIE GET AWAY WITH CHARGING TEN BUCKS A DRINK.

BUT HERE AT KADIE'S MY DRINKS ARE ALWAYS FREE. THE SWEET OLD TRANSSEXUAL WOULD BREAK MY ARM IF I TRIED TO PAY. I'VE DONE HER FAVORS AND THERE'S NOBODY WHO KNOWS WHERE THE BODIES ARE BURIED.

NOBODY BUT ME.

KADIE'S IS MY KIND OF JOINT. COUNTRY. AND I DON'T MEAN THAT TOUCHY-FEELY *"YOU PUT ME ON A NATURAL HIGH"* GARBAGE THEY'RE PASSING OFF AS COUNTRY THESE DAYS. NO, AT KADIE'S IT'S THE OLD STUFF. IT'S CONWAY AND TAMMY AND MERLE, FROM BACK BEFORE THEY WENT ALL SQUISHY. SONGS TO DRINK TO AND TO CRY TO.

I'M HIT SQUARE IN THE CHEST WITH THE PUMPED-UP-ALL-THE-WAY BASS OF EMMYLOU BELTING OUT *"DRIVING WHEEL."*

MUST BE NANCY UP ON STAGE.

THAT'S HER FAVORITE SONG TO SHAKE IT TO.

...DIDN'T MEAN IT LORD I DIDN'T MEAN IT I DON'T KNOW WHAT GOT INTO ME YOU KNOW I LOVE YOU, DARLING...

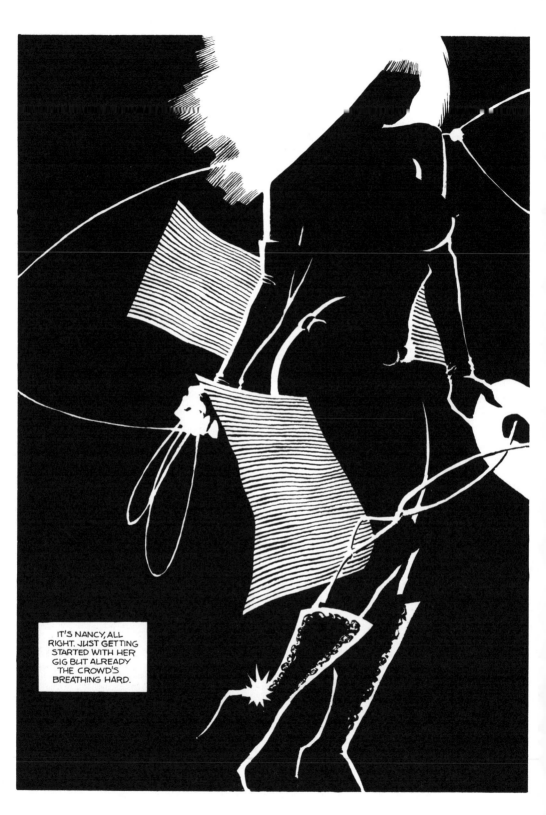

IT'S NANCY, ALL RIGHT. JUST GETTING STARTED WITH HER GIG BUT ALREADY THE CROWD'S BREATHING HARD.

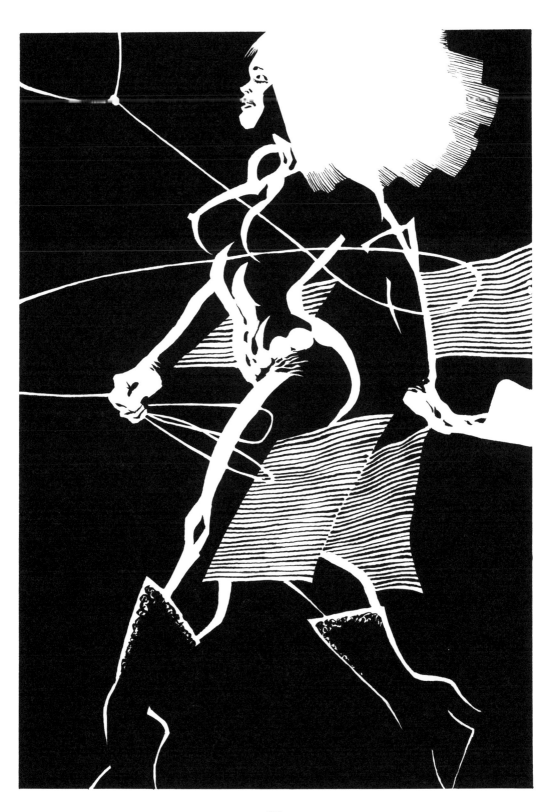

PLENTY OF NIGHTS I'VE DROOLED OVER NANCY, SHOULDER TO SHOULDER WITH ALL THE OTHER LOSERS LIKE ME.

BUT THAT'S NOT WHAT I'M LOOKING FOR TONIGHT.

I'M LOOKING FOR SOMETHING SMALL AND HAIRY.

THUMP

AAAK!

TAKE IT EASY, WEEVIL. I'M HERE TO DO YOU A FAVOR. IT'S MONEY IN YOUR POCKET.

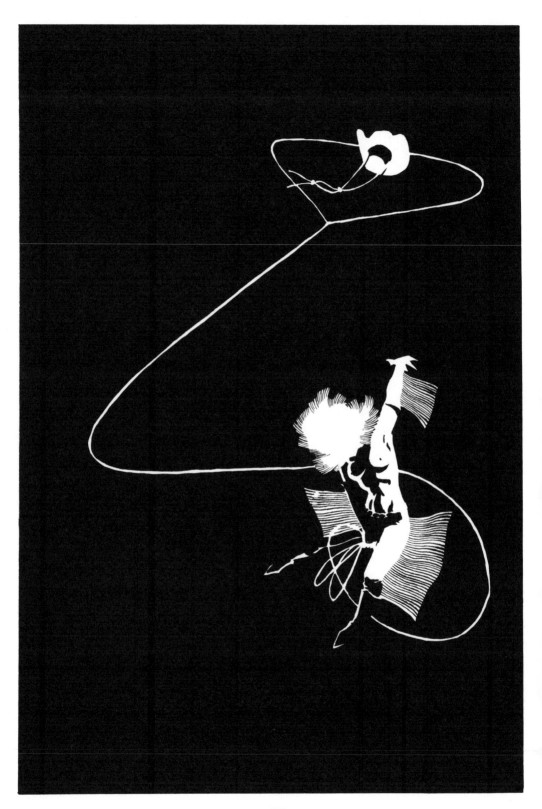

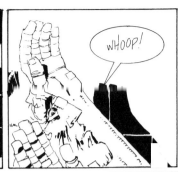

AW, HELL. THE
SUN'S UP.

NOW I GOT TO
GO AND FIND ME
A PLACE TO
SACK OUT.

AND HERE I
WAS JUST
GETTING
WARMED UP.
DAMN.

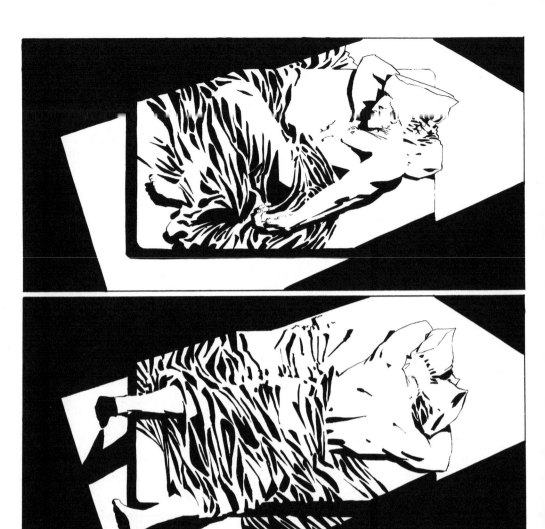

NO GOOD TRYING TO SLEEP. AND IT'S NOT THE STREET NOISE OR THE STENCH OF THIS NINE-DOLLAR FLOP, EITHER. I'M JUST TOO EXCITED. I CAN'T EVER SLEEP WHEN I'M EXCITED.

NO GAME ON T.V. NOTHING TO DO BUT SIT AND WAIT FOR THE DAMN SUN AND ALL THE PRYING EYES TO GET OUT OF THE WAY.

I HATE THE SUN.

AND THE EYES.

THE AIR COOLS. THE SOUNDS CHANGE. THE SUITS AND BRIEFCASES SCURRY TO THEIR FORTRESSES AND BOLT THEIR DOORS AND BALANCE THEIR CHECKBOOKS AND IGNORE THE SCREAMS AND TRY NOT TO THINK ABOUT WHO REALLY OWNS SIN CITY.

MY HANDS ARE SHAKING LIKE A KID'S AT CHRISTMAS. THE YEARS FALL AWAY, JUST SO MANY CHUNKS OF DEAD FLESH.

AND THERE'S BLOOD IN MY HANDS, IN MY ARMS, POUNDING BETWEEN MY EARS AND PUSHING ME FORWARD AND TELLING ME I'LL NEVER BE TIRED AGAIN...

NOoo NO MORE GHAAAGG

...AND THERE'S NO THINKING AND NO NEED FOR IT. THE INSTINCTS TAKE OVER, WHITE HOT, THE ANIMAL IN ME I TRIED TO DROWN IN BOOZE AND BLOODY BRAWLS, HE'S BACK, HE'S BACK AND HE'S HOWLING, HE'S LAUGHING OUT LOUD, HE'S CRAZY WITH THE PURE SWEET HATE OF IT ALL...

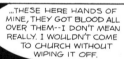

BY WAY OF A FOR INSTANCE, I KILLED THREE MEN TONIGHT. I TORTURED THEM FIRST.

YOU MIGHT SAY I BEEN WORKING MY WAY UP THE FOOD CHAIN. THE FIRST TWO, THEY WERE MINNOWS, SMALL-TIME MESSENGERS----BUT IT WAS CONNELLY--THE MONEY MAN--WHO FINGERED YOU, PADRE.

GHKCHAKK

YOU KNOW WHAT THAT SOUND MEANS. SIT DOWN.

DEAR LORD, MAN. THIS IS A HOUSE OF GOD.

JUST GIVE ME A DAMN NAME.

...ROARK.

ROARK?. YOU ARE REALLY PUSHING YOUR LUCK, TRYING TO FEED ME GARBAGE LIKE THIS.

IT CAN'T BE THAT BIG...

FIND OUT FOR YOURSELF, YOU SORRY BASTARD! THERE'S A FARM OUT AT NORTH CROSS AND LENNOX. IT'S ALL THERE. FIND OUT FOR YOURSELF--AND WHILE YOU'RE AT IT--

--ASK YOURSELF IF THAT CORPSE OF A SLUT IS WORTH DYING FOR.

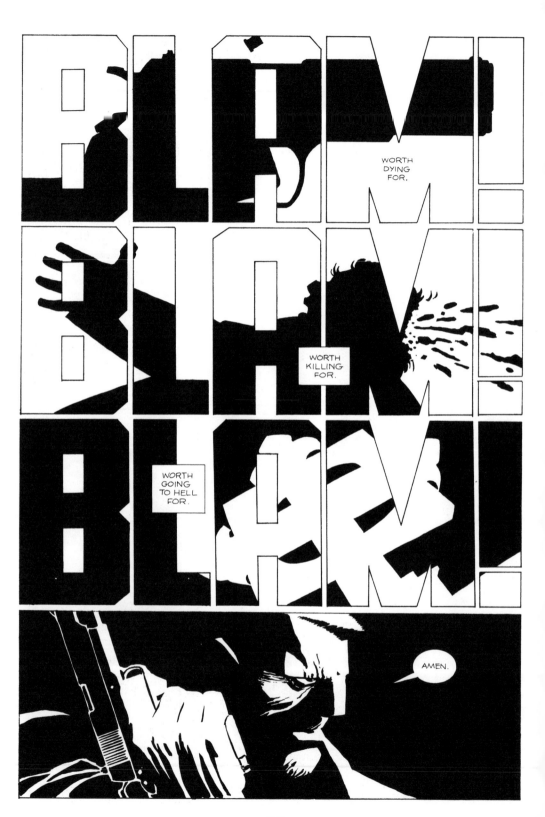

THERE ISN'T MUCH BETTER IN LIFE THAN A SMOKE WHEN YOU HAVEN'T HAD ONE IN A WHILE.

LIKE AFTER A MOVIE. OR AFTER CHURCH...

...I JUST MURDERED A PRIEST...

...HIS KEYS SAY THE PADRE DROVE A MERCEDES...

...OR AT LEAST WHAT THEY'RE PASSING OFF AS A MERCEDES, THESE DAYS.

MODERN CARS. THEY ALL LOOK LIKE ELECTRIC SHAVERS.

HNH?

SKREEEEEEEE

76

SIN CITY FALLS AWAY BEHIND ME, NOISY AND UGLY AS ALL HELL. THE MERCEDES HUMS AND HANDLES LIKE A DREAM. SHE MAY LOOK LIKE SOME JAP DESIGNED HER, BUT THE ENGINE'S A BEAUTY.

MY HEAD STARTS TO CLEAR. THINGS START TO MAKE SENSE.

THAT WASN'T GOLDIE BACK THERE. I LET MYSELF GET CONFUSED AGAIN. IT'S OKAY WHEN I SMELL THINGS THAT AREN'T THERE OR EVEN WHEN I HEAR THINGS. BUT IT'S PRETTY SERIOUS WHEN I SEE THINGS.

IT'S MY OWN FAULT AND NOBODY ELSE'S THAT I GOT CONFUSED. I WOULD'VE BEEN ALL RIGHT IF I TOOK MY MEDICINE WHEN I SHOULD HAVE.

I'VE BEEN HAVING SO MUCH FUN I FORGOT TO TAKE MY MEDICINE.

THAT WASN'T GOLDIE BACK THERE. GOLDIE IS DEAD AND THAT'S THE WHOLE REASON I'VE BEEN DOING WHAT I'VE BEEN DOING.

I FORGOT TO TAKE MY MEDICINE.

WHEN YOU'VE GOT A CONDITION IT'S BAD TO FORGET YOUR MEDICINE.

GULP

TWO MILES FROM THE FARM I SPOT A DINER AND LEAVE THE MERCEDES IN THE PARKING LOT AND MOVE AHEAD ON FOOT. IF THERE'S ANYTHING TO WHAT THE PADRE TOLD ME I'VE GOT TO PLAY THIS CAREFUL.

EVEN IF IT MEANS CUTTING THROUGH THE WOODS AT NIGHT.

I HATE THE WOODS AT NIGHT. ESPECIALLY THE SOUNDS. PEOPLE ARE ALWAYS TALKING ABOUT NATURE LIKE IT'S ALL SWEET AND FRIENDLY. ALL I CAN FIGURE IS THEY NEVER SPENT A NIGHT TIED TO A TREE IN THE WOODS.

EVER SINCE CAMP I'VE HATED THE WOODS.

THERE ISN'T MUCH ELSE THAT SCARES ME.

...THAT COLD THING. IT CREEPS INTO MY GUT AND TELLS ME ONE MORE TIME IT WON'T LET GO. I MAY GET CONFUSED SOMETIMES, BUT THE COLD THING, IT'S NEVER WRONG AND I'VE LEARNED TO TRUST IT.

MAYBE IT'S SOMETHING I SMELL OR HEAR OR SPOT OUT OF THE CORNER OF MY EYE, SOMETHING I'M TOO DUMB TO NOTICE. BUT HERE IT IS AGAIN, THAT ICEBALL WHERE MY STOMACH OUGHT TO BE.

THIS IS A BAD PLACE, THIS FARM. PEOPLE HAVE DIED HERE.

THE WRONG WAY.

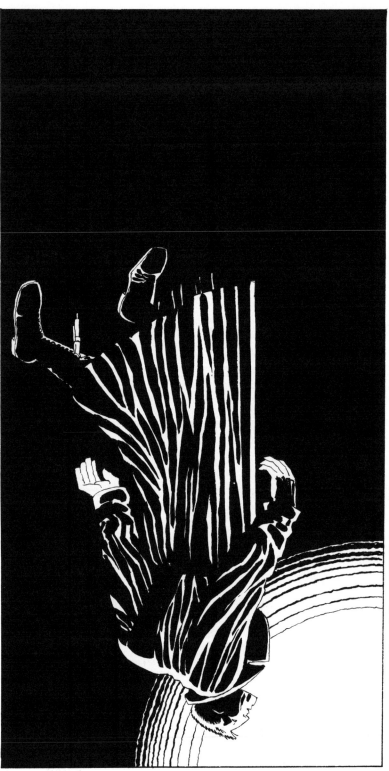

FOR A WHILE IT'S OUTER SPACE WITH NO STARS IN IT, COLD AND BLACK AND BOTTOMLESS. I TUMBLE, WEIGHTLESS AS A GHOST.

FOR A WHILE I'VE GOT NO BRAIN AND NO BODY AND THAT'S FINE BY ME.

THEN THE BROKEN BITS START WITH THEIR NAGGING. THE JAGGED LITTLE BASTARDS DANCE LIKE LEPRECHAUNS, PULLING TOGETHER IN A BULLIES' CIRCLE, LAUGHING AT ME, TELLING ME I'M AN EVEN BIGGER LOSER THAN I EVER THOUGHT I WAS.

THEY PLAY IT BACK FOR ME LIKE A MOVIE ON REWIND-- FROM THE SUNBURST OF THE SLEDGEHAMMER HITTING MY FACE--BACK TO THE SOFT CHILLY SKIN OF THE GODDESS WHO WAS MURDERED IN MY BED.

I BLEW IT, GOLDIE. I FOUND YOUR KILLER BUT HE WAS BETTER THAN ME, TOO QUIET AND TOO QUICK, A KILLER BORN. HE TOOK ME OUT LIKE I WAS A GIRL SCOUT. HE DIDN'T EVEN BREAK A SWEAT...

...BUT IF I'M DOING ALL THIS THINKING, THAT MEANS I'M STILL ALIVE, DOESN'T IT?

WHY DIDN'T HE FINISH THE JOB?...OR IS THIS THE HELL I'VE SPENT MY WHOLE LIFE EARNING, FALLING, FOREVER FALLING, NEVER KNOWING?

THEN THE HURT COMES. THE LIVING HURT. STREAKING FROM BEHIND MY EYES. FINDING PLACES TO HAVE ITS FUN.

A SMELL HITS MY NOSTRILS, HARD, BURNING, ANTISEPTIC.

LIGHT GROWS.

I DIVE FOR IT.

98

DAMES. SOMETIMES ALL THEY GOT TO DO IS LET IT OUT AND A FEW BUCKETS LATER THERE'S NO WAY YOU'D EVER KNOW.

I WATCH LUCILLE SLIDE EVERY GORGEOUS INCH OF HERSELF INTO MY COAT. I SHAKE MY HEAD FOR WHAT MUST BE THE MILLIONTH TIME. HARDWARE LIKE SHE'S GOT AND LUCILLE'S A DYKE. IT'S A DAMN CRIME.

BUT I DON'T SAY A WORD ABOUT THAT. I PIPED UP AT HER ONCE THAT MAYBE SHE OUGHT TO GET TREATMENT OR SOMETHING AND SHE HAULED OFF AND NAILED ME WITH A PUNCH THAT SHOWED ME THERE WAS PLENTY OF MUSCLE UNDER ALL THAT HEAVEN.

BUT THAT WAS YEARS AGO AND IT HASN'T GOT ANYTHING TO DO WITH GETTING OUT OF HERE.

YOU'VE BROUGHT US SOME BIG TROUBLE THIS TIME, MARV. WHOEVER'S BEHIND ALL THIS HAS GOT HIS CONNECTIONS-- RIGHT IN THE DEPARTMENT. ANY LEADS?

NUFF

YEAH, I DID SOME NOSING AROUND.

ONE GUY I TALKED TO, HE TOLD ME IT WAS *ROARK* RUNNING THE SHOW.

THAT'S GOT TO BE BULLSHIT.

JUST TELLING YOU WHAT I BEEN TOLD. WHUFF

WELL, WHOEVER IT IS, HE KNEW I WAS CHECKING OUT THAT HOOKER ALMOST BEFORE I DID.

WHAT HOOKER?

THE ONE YOU'VE BEEN OBSESSING OVER. THE DEAD ONE.

GOLDIE.

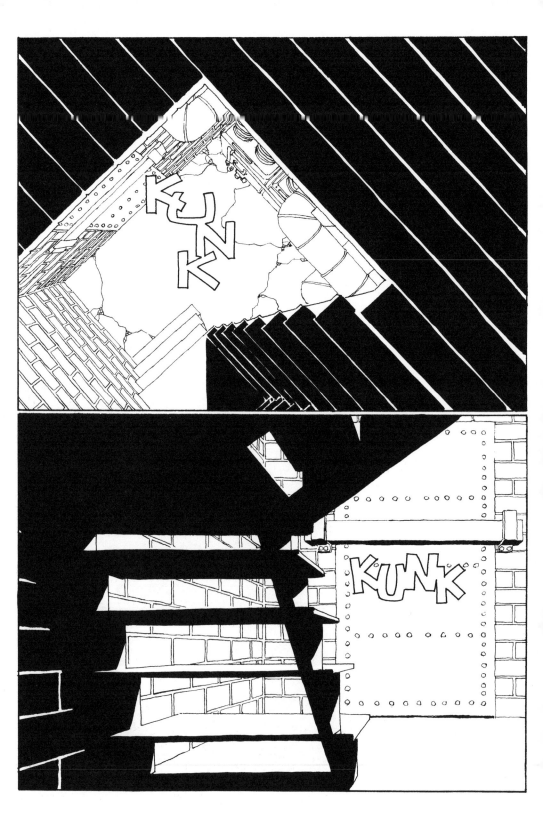

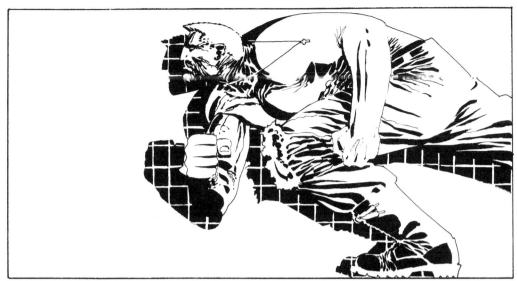

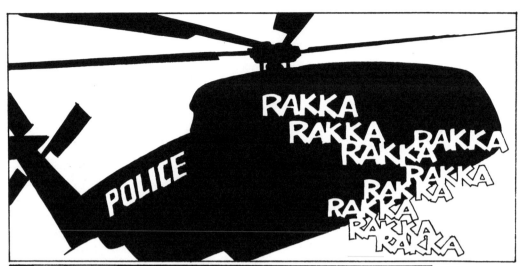

THE WIND OFF THE DESERT GOES COLD.

LUCILLE'S A KITTEN UNDER MY ARM, SOFT AND WEIGHTLESS AND WARM.

BUT I KNOW GLADYS WILL BE COLD, COLDER THAN THE WIND, COLD AND READY AND BEGGING FOR IT.

SWEET GLADYS.

...THEY'RE DONE CHECKING THE HOUSE...THEY'RE COMING THIS WAY...BASTARDS. I'LL SHOW THEM...

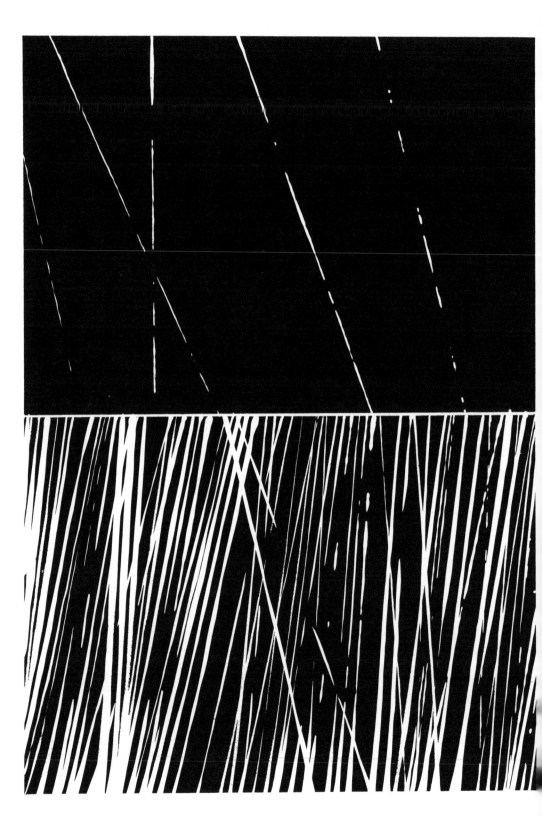

128

RAIN DOESN'T COME TO SIN CITY REAL OFTEN. AND WHEN IT DOES, IT'S USUALLY PRETTY LAME STUFF. WARM AS SWEAT AND LUCKY IF IT GETS TO THE PAVEMENT BEFORE IT EVAPORATES.

BUT MAYBE TWICE A YEAR THE DESERT SKY REALLY COUGHS IT UP AND SPITS IT OUT. A COLD, MEAN TORRENT THAT TURNS THE STREETS TO GLASS AND CHILLS YOU TO THE BONE.

MOST PEOPLE HATE THE RAIN WHEN IT'S NASTY LIKE THIS. BUT ME, I LOVE IT. IT HELPS ME THINK.

I'M NOT REAL SMART, BUT I FEEL A WHOLE LOT SMARTER WHEN EVERYTHING GOES SLICK AND EVERYBODY SKITTERS OFF THE STREETS AND GETS OUT OF MY WAY.

I LOVE THE RAIN. I LOVE THE ICY WAY IT CREEPS DOWN MY NECK. THE WAY THE AIR GOES ELECTRIC AND EVERYTHING SEEMS SO CLEAR.

YOU BREATHE IN AND YOUR NOSTRILS WORK.

THAT'S WHAT I DO. I BREATHE IN AND I JUST LET MY FEET TAKE ME WHEREVER THEY WANT.

AND I THINK.

MY EYES STILL WATCH OUT FOR A SQUAD CAR OR A BEAT COP BUT MY BRAIN GOES OFF ON ITS OWN DEEP INSIDE SPREADING OUT THE PUZZLE PIECES ONE MORE TIME, TRYING TO FIND TWO THAT'LL FIT TOGETHER, LOOKING FOR SOME HINT OF THE BIG PICTURE.

BUT MOSTLY I KEEP COMING BACK TO THAT COP I JUST KILLED AND WHAT HE TOLD ME.

HE WAS A TOUGH ONE AND I WAS PRETTY STEAMED ABOUT WHAT HE DONE TO LUCILLE ANYWAY SO I TOOK MY TIME WITH THE SON OF A BITCH. IT WASN'T UNTIL I SHOWED HIM ALL THOSE PIECES OF HIMSELF THAT HE SAID WHAT HE SAID. THEN ALL OF A SUDDEN HE WAS THE ONE DOING THE LAUGHING BECAUSE HE SAW THE LOOK ON MY FACE AND HE DIED KNOWING I WISHED TO GOD HE'D KEPT HIS MOUTH SHUT AFTER ALL.

IT WAS JUST A NAME BUT I HAVEN'T STOPPED SHAKING SINCE I HEARD IT. AND THE RAIN ISN'T THE REASON I'M SHAKING, EITHER.

JUST A NAME. BACK WHEN THE PRIEST SAID IT I FIGURED HE WAS JERKING MY CHAIN. BUT HEARING IT FROM THE COP I KNEW IT COULDN'T BE A COINCIDENCE.

JUST A NAME.

ROARK.

ROARK!

DAMN IT!

EVERY INCH OF ME WANTS TO TURN TAIL, TO SNEAK INTO THE BACK OF A TRUCK OR HOP A FREIGHT CAR AND HAUL OUT OF TOWN. I WANT TO RUN, RUN LIKE HELL, TO CRAWL INTO A CAVE SOMEWHERE AND FORGET ABOUT GOLDIE AND LUCILLE AND SILENT, DEADLY KEVIN.

ROARK. DAMN IT.

I'M AS GOOD AS DEAD.

I'M AS GOOD AS DEAD.

AND IT'S NOT THAT I'M ANY KIND OF HERO THAT MAKES ME STAY. HEROES DON'T GO WEAK IN THE KNEES AND FEEL LIKE THROWING UP OR CURLING UP INTO A LITTLE BALL AND CRYING LIKE A BABY.

AND EVEN THOUGH MY LIFE WOULD BE NOTHING BUT AN ENDLESS GREY HELL OF BOOZE AND BRAWLS LIKE IT WAS BEFORE, I'M MORE SCARED OF DYING THAN I AM OF LIVING.

NO, I'M NO HERO. NOT BY A LONG SHOT. I JUST KNOW GOLDIE WON'T LET ME OFF SO EASY. NO MATTER WHERE I GO I'LL SMELL HER ANGEL SMELL. I'LL SEE THAT MOUTH AND THOSE EYES AND THAT PERFECT, PERFECT BODY. I'LL HEAR HER AND I'LL TASTE HER AND I'LL KNOW IT WAS ME, ONLY ME, WHO COULD HAVE SET THINGS RIGHT.

YOU WERE SCARED, WEREN'T YOU, GOLDIE? SOMEBODY WANTED YOU DEAD AND YOU KNEW IT. SO YOU HIT THE SALOONS, THE BAD PLACES, LOOKING FOR THE BIGGEST, MEANEST LUG AROUND AND FINDING ME.

LOOKING FOR PROTECTION AND PAYING FOR IT WITH YOUR BODY AND MORE --WITH LOVE, WITH WILD FIRE, MAKING ME FEEL LIKE A KING, LIKE A DAMN WHITE KNIGHT.

LIKE A HERO.

WHAT A LAUGH.

YOU WANTED ME TO KEEP YOU SAFE BUT WHEN THAT BASTARD CAME TO KILL YOU I WAS STONE DRUNK.

BLACKED OUT.

USELESS.

I OWE YOU, GOLDIE. I OWE YOU AND I'M GOING TO PAY UP. SO GOING AFTER ROARK MEANS DYING, WIN OR LOSE. HELL. DYING WILL BE NOTHING. I'LL DIE LAUGHING IF I KNOW I'VE DONE THIS ONE THING RIGHT.

BUT FIRST I HAVE TO KNOW THE WHY OF IT. THE CONNECTION BETWEEN ROARK AND YOU AND THE FARM-BOY CANNIBAL WHO KILLED YOU.

THEN I'LL KNOW EXACTLY WHAT TO DO AND WHO TO DO IT TO.

I LOVE THE RAIN.

IT HELPS ME THINK.

133

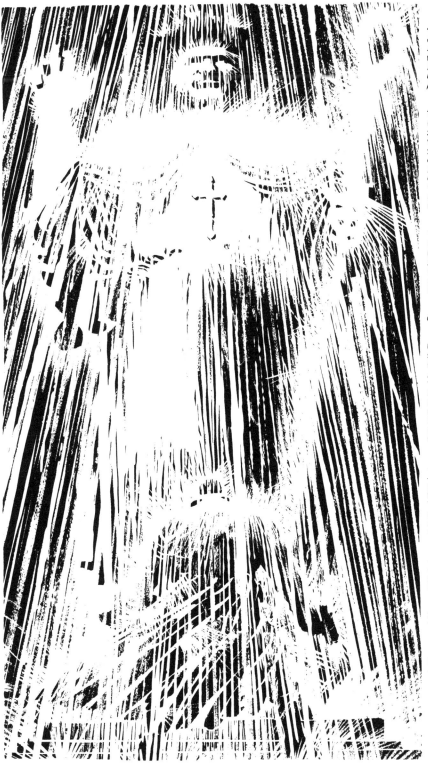

"SAINT PATRICK," THEY CALL HIM BUT IT'S JUST A NICKNAME. THE POPE HASN'T GOTTEN AROUND TO MAKING IT OFFICIAL. NOT YET, ANYWAY.

THE ROARK FAMILY HAS OWNED SIN CITY SINCE THE DAYS OF WAGON TRAINS AND SIX-GUNS. OVER THE GENERATIONS THEIR MILLIONS HAVE GROWN TO BILLIONS. THEY'RE KIND OF LIKE OUR OWN ROYAL FAMILY.

THIS PARTICULAR GENERATION PRODUCED A UNITED STATES SENATOR, A STATE ATTORNEY GENERAL--AND PATRICK HENRY ROARK.

CARDINAL ROARK.

BACK IN SCHOOL THE SISTERS WOULD NEVER SHUT UP ABOUT HIM. MAN OF THE CLOTH. WAR HERO IN THE MEDICAL CORPS. PHILANTHROPIST. EDUCATOR. COULD'VE BECOME PRESIDENT BUT HE CHOSE TO SERVE GOD.

AND ALONG THE WAY HE JUST HAPPENED TO BECOME THE MOST POWERFUL MAN IN THE STATE. HE'S BROUGHT DOWN MAYORS AND GOTTEN GOVERNORS ELECTED.

AND HERE HE'S GOING TO GET KILLED IN THE NAME OF A DEAD HOOKER.

I'M GETTING USED TO THE IDEA.

MORE AND MORE I'M LIKING THE SOUND OF IT.

THEN IT HITS ME LIKE A KICK IN THE NUTS. WHAT IF I'M WRONG?

I'VE GOT A CONDITION. I GET CONFUSED SOMETIMES. AND WITH LUCILLE DEAD I CAN'T GET MY MEDICINE.

WHAT IF I'M IMAGINING THINGS? LIKE I DID WHEN I THOUGHT GOLDIE ATTACKED ME AFTER SHE WAS ALREADY DEAD?

WHAT IF I IMAGINED ALL OF THIS? FROM GOLDIE'S SLOW SMILE TO THE COP FINGERING ROARK? WHAT IF I'VE FINALLY TURNED INTO WHAT THEY ALWAYS SAID I WAS GOING TO TURN INTO--A MANIAC, A PSYCHO KILLER?

CAN'T KILL A MAN WITHOUT KNOWING FOR SURE YOU OUGHT TO.

I'VE GOT TO KNOW FOR SURE.

THE RAIN'S SPUTTERED TO A STOP AND THE STREETS HAVE COME BACK TO LIFE BY THE TIME I MAKE MY WAY TO OLD TOWN.

THE MERCHANDISE IS ON DISPLAY, NEVER MIND THE COLD. PRETTY SOON EVERYTHING FROM PICKUPS TO LIMOS WILL BE PULLING IN AND BUSINESS WILL BE BOOMING.

OLD TOWN IS WHY NOBODY CALLS THIS BURG "BASIN CITY" LIKE IT SAYS ON THE MAPS.

IT WAS SAINT PATRICK'S GREAT-GRANDFATHER WHO MADE IT HAPPEN. BACK THEN THIS WAS A GOLD RUSH TOWN ON ITS WAY TO BECOMING A GHOST TOWN.

THEN OLD MAN ROARK GOT HIMSELF AN IDEA.

HE SPENT EVERY SILVER DOLLAR HE HAD, IMPORTING TOP HOOKERS FROM FRANCE AND PLACES LIKE THAT.

WORD GOT OUT AND PRETTY SOON SIN CITY WAS THE HOTTEST STOP IN THE WEST. PEOPLE WOULD COME FROM MILES AROUND.

THEY STILL DO AND IT'S EASY TO SEE WHY. OLD TOWN'S KEPT ITS TRADITIONS, HANDED DOWN FROM GORGEOUS MOTHER TO GORGEOUS DAUGHTER.

FOR AN HOUR OR SO I ASK AROUND ABOUT GOLDIE. I DON'T GET ANY ANSWERS BUT I KNOW I'M BOUND TO. LUCILLE SAID GOLDIE WAS A HOOKER AND IF SHE WAS SHE HAS ROOTS HERE. FRIENDS.

MAYBE EVEN FAMILY.

140

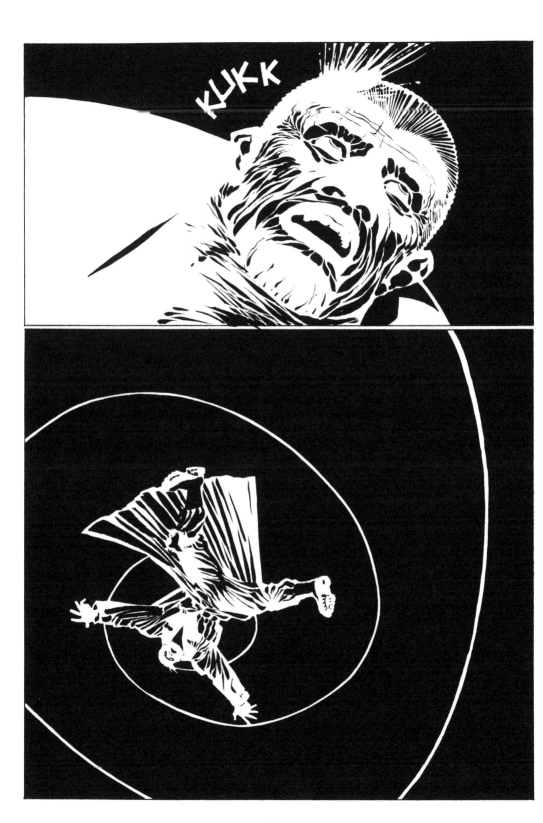

141

KOFF

GOLDIE. YEAH. SURE. RIGHT.

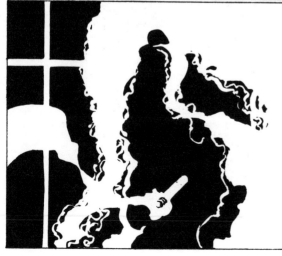

IT'S OKAY, GOLDIE. I GOT NOBODY TO BLAME BUT ME. I BROUGHT ALL THIS ON MYSELF AND THERE'S NO USE DENYING IT. I HAVEN'T HAD ANYTHING TO EAT OR GOTTEN ANY SLEEP OR TAKEN MY MEDICINE FOR DAYS NOW. SO IT'S NO WONDER I'M SEEING THINGS, IS IT?

144

147

I WIPE THE BLOOD OFF AND I TAKE A DEEP BREATH AND I TAKE A GOOD LONG LOOK AT THE MONSTER IN THE MIRROR.

DON'T SCREW UP THIS TIME, MARV. IT'S TOO IMPORTANT. RIGHT NOW, WHILE YOU'RE ALONE, FEEL THE FEAR AND GET PAST IT. GO AHEAD. SHAKE LIKE A JUNKIE. LET YOUR HEART CRAWL UP YOUR THROAT. LET YOUR STOMACH SQUEEZE ITSELF INTO A GOLF BALL, INTO ONE OF THOSE BLACK HOLES THAT SUCKS EVERYTHING INTO IT.

THINK ABOUT DYING. THINK HARD. PICTURE IT. A BULLET THROUGH YOUR BRAIN AND THAT'S IF YOU'RE LUCKY, GETTING IT THAT QUICK.

BUT IT'S JUST AS LIKELY GOING TO BE THE SLOW WAY. A LONG, BAD JOKE OF A TRIAL AND A LONGER WAIT IN A CELL UNTIL THEY STRAP YOU INTO THAT CHAIR AND A MILLION VOLTS SEND **YOU** STRAIGHT TO **HELL AND THEY'LL CALL YOU A PSYCHO** KILLER WHO GOT WHAT WAS COMING TO HIM.

PICTURE IT. FEEL IT. GET USED TO IT. THEN PUT IT BACK INSIDE WHERE IT BELONGS. YOU'VE GOT SOME PEOPLE TO KILL. AND IF YOU DO IT RIGHT IT WON'T MATTER WHAT ANYBODY SAYS. YOU'LL GO TO YOUR GRAVE A WINNER.

I THROW UP A COUPLE OF TIMES AND THEN I'M READY.

153

I TRY NOT TO LOOK AT HER TOO MUCH. IT MAKES IT WORSE WHEN I DO. BUT WHEN I CLOSE MY EYES FOR TOO LONG IT HAPPENS ANYWAY. I GET CONFUSED AND START THINKING SHE'S GOLDIE. SHE'S GOT THE SMELL AND THE VOICE JUST LIKE SHE'S GOT THE LOOKS. EVERYTHING'S TELLING ME SHE'S GOLDIE AND I HAVE TO KEEP REMINDING MYSELF SHE ISN'T. GOLDIE'S DEAD AND THE ANGEL SITTING NEXT TO ME, SHE'S WENDY. GOLDIE'S TWIN SISTER.

AND SHE'S ONE TOUGH BIRD. SHE'S BOUNCED ME AROUND A PARKING LOT WITH HER CUTE LITTLE PORSCHE, SHE'S SHOT ME AND PISTOL-WHIPPED ME AND IT TOOK SOME FAST TALKING TO KEEP HER FROM BLOWING MY BRAINS OUT.

SHE'S WENDY. GOLDIE'S TWIN SISTER.

I CAN'T LET MYSELF GET CONFUSED ABOUT THAT.

154

I KNOW THAT SOUNDS CRAZY.

NO, IT DOESN'T. GOLDIE WORKED THE CLERGY.

"GOLDIE WORKED THE CLERGY"... JUST LIKE THAT A WHOPPER OF A PUZZLE PIECE FALLS SMACK IN MY LAP. I'M TOO DUMB TO PUT THE WHOLE PICTURE TOGETHER YET, BUT...

...BUT SHE FIRES UP TWO CIGARETTES AND HANDS ME ONE AND I TASTE HER LIPSTICK ON IT AND SUDDENLY MY HEART'S POUNDING SO LOUD I CAN'T HEAR ANYTHING ELSE. I WANT TO CRY AND I WANT TO LAUGH AT THE CRAZINESS OF IT ALL BUT MOSTLY I WANT TO REACH OVER AND TOUCH HER AND TASTE GOLDIE'S SWEAT ONE MORE TIME.

BUT SHE ISN'T GOLDIE.

HONK

SKREECHH

157

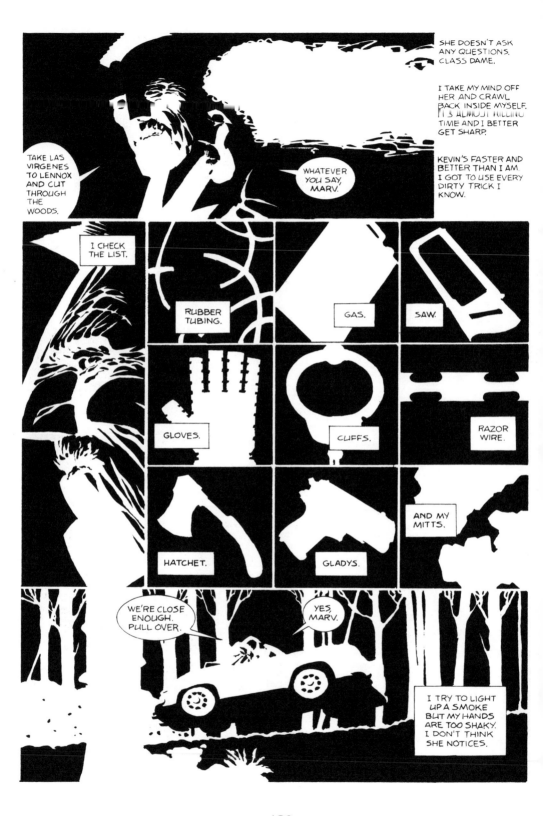

HER EYES ARE BURNING HOLES THROUGH ME BUT STILL SHE DOESN'T ASK. SHE KNOWS I'M THE ONLY CHANCE SHE HAS.

STAY HERE. KEEP THE ENGINE RUNNING. IF I'M NOT BACK IN TWENTY MINUTES, GET THE HELL OUT OF HERE AND DON'T LOOK BACK.

KILL HIM FOR ME, MARV. KILL HIM GOOD.

I WON'T LET YOU DOWN, GOLDIE. I PROMISED.

IT ISN'T LONG
BEFORE I BREAK
INTO A RUN. I CAN'T
HELP MYSELF.

NO SHAKING, NOW.
NO COLD SWEAT. NO
DOUBTS. THE FEAR
GOT OUT FOR A
LITTLE WHILE THERE
BUT NOW IT'S
CRAWLED BACK IN,
FAR AWAY, A SMALL
COLD THING LOST
IN A BELLY THAT'S
FULL OF FIRE.

EVEN THE WOODS
DON'T SCARE ME
ANYMORE BECAUSE
I'M JUST ONE MORE
PREDATOR AND I'M
BIGGER AND
MEANER THAN
THE REST.

ALL I'VE EVER
BEEN GOOD AT IS
KILLING SO I
MIGHT AS WELL
ENJOY IT.

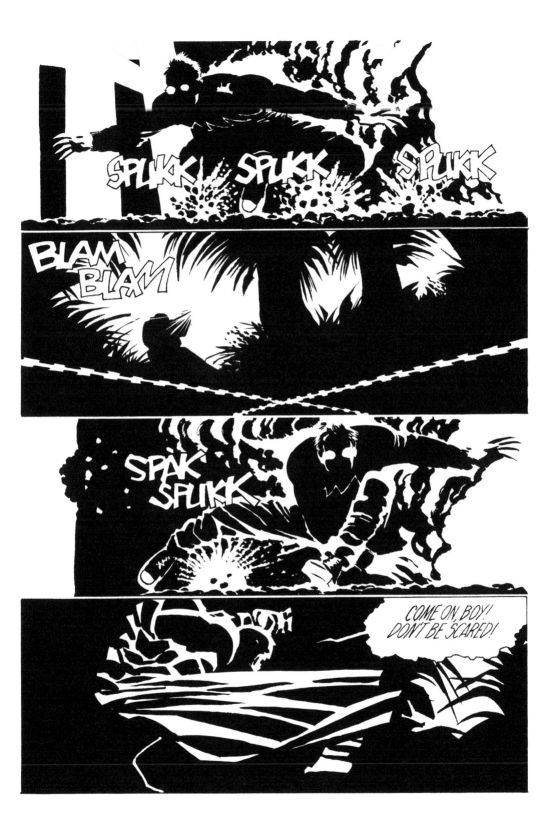

IS THAT THE BEST YOU CAN DO, CREEP?

THAT'S RIGHT--
GET PERSONAL--
GET *CLOSE* --

--I CAN
TAKE IT--

FOR A WHILE I JUST TRY TO
SLOW MY HEART DOWN AND BREATHE
THE FIRE OUT OF MY LUNGS. MY
MUSCLES MAKE ME A THOUSAND
PROMISES OF PAIN TO COME. IT'LL
BE A ROUGH MORNING IF I'M
ALIVE TO SEE IT.

THE NIGHT'S ALL
WEIRD AND QUIET.
SO QUIET THE
CRICKETS SEEM
LOUD.

KEFF

THEN THERE'S A
GENTLE FLAP OF
FABRIC AND LIGHT
FOOTSTEPS ON THE
GRASS.

AND THAT
SCENT.

MAYBE A HALF HOUR LATER...

I'LL TELL YOU, I AM GOOD AND BUSHED. AND IT WASN'T OUR FIGHT THAT DID ME IN, EITHER. IT WAS ALL THAT *SAWING* AND *TYING*. IT'S NOT AS EASY AS IT LOOKS.

BUT IF I DO SAY SO MYSELF, I THINK I DID A PRETTY NEAT JOB OF IT. AND IT'S A GOOD THING I BOUGHT ALL THAT EXTRA *TUBING*. A LOT OF THEM *BROKE*--

--WHEN I WAS FIXING THE *TORNIQUETS*.

IT WOULD'VE BEEN A *MESS* AROUND HERE IF I HADN'T HAD SOME TO SPARE. STILL AND ALL, I GOT TO ADMIT THERE WAS A SPURT OR TWO.

HELL, I MIGHT AS WELL COME CLEAN. I WANTED A SPURT OR TWO. TO GET THE SCENT IN THE AIR. TO GET A FRIEND OF *YOURS* TO COME RUNNING.

GRRRRR

PRRRRR

AND WHAT DO YOU KNOW. HERE HE COMES NOW.

LET'S SEE WHAT HAPPENS IF I LOOSEN UP ONE OF THESE HERE TORNIQUETS.

178

179

...NOT EVEN
AT THE END

NOT EVEN WHEN **THE MUTT'S**
HAD HIS FILL AND KEVIN'S GUTS
ARE LYING ALL OVER THE PLACE
AND SOMEHOW THE BASTARD IS
STILL ALIVE, STILL STARING AT
ME.

NOT EVEN WHEN I
GRAB THE SAW AND
FINISH THE JOB.

*HE NEVER
SCREAMS!*

ON THE WAY BACK INTO TOWN I PULL OVER TO A TRUCK STOP AND USE THE PAY PHONE TO PUT IN A CALL TO KADIE'S AND ASK NANCY TO GET HER CLOTHES ON AND MEET ME AT HER PLACE. SHE SAYS YES, LIKE ALWAYS.

THERE ISN'T MUCH OF ANYTHING NANCY WOULDN'T DO FOR ME, NOT SINCE A YEAR BACK WHEN A FRAT BOY ROUGHED HER UP AND I STRAIGHTENED HIM OUT BUT GOOD. MAYBE I WENT A LITTLE TOO FAR, BUT I WAS PLENTY STEAMED, SEEING HER CRYING LIKE THAT.

IT REALLY GETS MY GOAT WHEN GUYS ROUGH UP DAMES.

HI, NANCY. GOT ANY BEERS?

SURE, MARV. WHO'S THE BABE?

...SO WHAT DO YOU WANT ME TO DO WITH HER?

SHE POPS OPEN AN ICE COLD LONG NECK. I INHALE IT. ON MY SECOND BEER I START FILLING HER IN. BY MY FIFTH ONE SHE'S UP TO SPEED.

WHILE SHE'S PATCHING ME UP NANCY RESTS MY HAND ON HER THIGH AND IT'S SOFT AND WARM BUT THAT'S NONE OF MY BUSINESS. AND IT WOULDN'T BUG ME LIKE IT DOES IF I DIDN'T FEEL SO DAMNED ALIVE.

SHE'LL COME AROUND IN A FEW HOURS. YOU TELL HER EVERYTHING'S OKAY BUT SHE HAS TO HAUL ON OUT OF TOWN. SHE COULD GET KILLED IF SHE DOESN'T.

I'LL TAKE HER TO THE AIRPORT MYSELF.

NO, THAT'S NO GOOD. THEY MIGHT HAVE IT WATCHED. YOUR BEST BET IS TO DRIVE HER ALL THE WAY TO SACRED OAKS. PUT HER ON A PLANE THERE. SHE'LL KICK UP A FUSS BUT TELL HER I SAID SHE OWES ME ONE. IT'S NOT TRUE BUT SHE'LL BELIEVE IT.

=URPP=

SHE SHOULD BE OKAY. THERE'S NO WAY THEY'LL =URPP= CONNECT HER TO ME. BUT ANYBODY WHO'S HAD ANYTHING TO DO WITH GOLDIE IS BOUND TO CATCH HEAT IN A BIG WAY. SO IT'S BETTER IF SHE'S GONE WHEN THEY COME CALLING.

KEFF

WHAT ABOUT YOU? ARE YOU LEAVING TOWN?

HELL, NO. I LIKE IT HERE. =URPP=

FIRST I WALK TWENTY BLOCKS WEST. THEY'LL BE FOLLOWING MY TRAIL BACKWARDS AND I DON'T WANT IT LEADING TO NANCY.

THEN I HOTWIRE A PARKED CAB AND STAY UNDER THE SPEED LIMITS, SO AS NOT TO GET ANY ATTENTION. THIS'D BE A DUMB TIME TO GET PULLED OVER.

THE WIND IS WARM ON MY FACE AND EVERYTHING'S SIMPLE AND CLEAR. I CAN'T HELP SMILING.

182

THE *MISSION.*

"CASTLE ROARK" IS WHAT SOME PEOPLE CALL IT AND IF YOU ASK ME THEY AREN'T WRONG. ROARK'S BEEN HOLED UP THERE FOR YEARS, SURROUNDED BY A SQUAD OF ARMED GUARDS, SITTING PRETTY WHILE MAYORS AND SENATORS AND GOVERNORS COME, HATS IN HAND, BEGGING FAVORS FROM MIGHTY SAINT PATRICK.

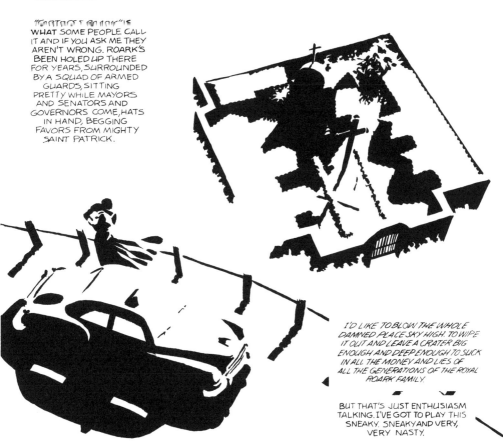

I'D LIKE TO BLOW THE WHOLE DAMNED PLACE SKY HIGH. TO WIPE IT OUT AND LEAVE A CRATER BIG ENOUGH AND DEEP ENOUGH TO SUCK IN ALL THE MONEY AND LIES OF ALL THE GENERATIONS OF THE ROYAL ROARK FAMILY.

BUT THAT'S JUST ENTHUSIASM TALKING. I'VE GOT TO PLAY THIS SNEAKY. SNEAKY AND VERY, VERY NASTY.

THIS IS IT, GOLDIE. WIN OR LOSE, IT'S ALL OVER TONIGHT.

I HOPE YOU DON'T MIND MY SAYING IT, BUT YOU'RE ONE HECK OF LOT SMALLER THAN I THOUGHT YOU'D BE. I MEAN, YOU ARE REALLY LITTLE.

"..OH, GOD!

YOU MONSTER! YOU MONSTER!

AT LEAST I DON'T GO AROUND EATING PEOPLE.

YOU DON'T UNDERSTAND HIM! YOU DON'T KNOW ANYTHING ABOUT HIM!

...YOU PROBABLY THINK HE COULDN'T TALK, DON'T YOU?

YOU'RE WRONG ABOUT THAT. HE HAD A VOICE LIKE AN ANGEL.

BUT HE SPOKE ONLY TO ME. ONLY TO ME.

AND NOW HE'S DEAD-- AND ALL BECAUSE OF ONE STUPID WHORE!

HER NAME WAS GOLDIE AND IT'S NOT A REAL GOOD IDEA FOR YOU TO TALK ABOUT HER THAT WAY WHILE I'M AROUND. JUST GIVE WITH THE SCOOP. THE WHOLE STORY. IF YOU DON'T I'LL START WITH YOUR FINGERS AND YOU'LL TALK ANYWAY.

...HE WAS JUST A BOY WHEN HE FIRST CAME TO ME--AND I WAS JUST A PRIEST. HE CAME TO GIVE CONFESSION...
...HE WAS A TORTURED SOUL. TORMENTED BY GUILT.

BUT THE EATING--IT FILLED HIM WITH WHITE LIGHT--WITH LOVE FOR EVERY LIVING THING. TEARFUL, HE SWORE TO ME THAT HE FELT THE TOUCH OF GOD ALMIGHTY!

"AT FIRST, I THOUGHT HE WAS INSANE. I TRIED TO COUNSEL HIM. TO CONTROL HIM."

"BUT, AS YEARS PASSED, KEVIN'S VOICE GREW RICHER, DEEPER, MORE *CERTAIN*--UNTIL IT FILLED ME WITH PLEASURE, JUST TO HEAR HIM SPEAK... JUST TO SHARE IN HIS ECSTACY..."

"...IN TIME, I BEGAN TO ENVY HIM. THE VOICE WAS NO LONGER ENOUGH. I COULD NO LONGER STAND TO THE SIDE, WHILE HE TOUCHED *HEAVEN*."

"DON'T LOOK AT ME THAT WAY. YOU DON'T KNOW. YOU JUST DON'T KNOW."

"I KNOW IT'S PRETTY DAMN WEIRD TO EAT PEOPLE."

"HE DIDN'T JUST EAT THEIR *BODIES*, YOU PIG! HE ATE THEIR *SOULS!* HE LOVED THEM IN A WAY THAT WAS ABSOLUTE AND CLEAN AND PERFECT!"

"AND YOU JOINED IN."

"YES... OH, YES..."

"THE WOMEN WERE *NOTHING*. WHORES. *NOBODY* MISSED THEM. NOBODY *CARED*. AND THEN THAT *ONE GIRL*--YOUR *GOLDIE*--ALMOST RUINED *EVERYTHING!*"

"SHE MUST HAVE SUSPECTED SOMETHING, AFTER THE FIRST FEW GIRLS. PERHAPS SHE SAW ONE OF THEM GETTING INTO MY LIMOUSINE..."

"...SHE FOLLOWED US..."

KEVIN WAS...ENGROSSED, WHEN SHE FOUND US. SHE MADE IT TO HER CAR AND ESCAPED.

SHE STAYED IN PUBLIC PLACES, THEN WITH YOU.

YOU WERE SO *CONVENIENT*. *NOBODY* WOULD BELIEVE A THUG LIKE YOU. YOU'D BROKEN A MAN'S JAW THAT SAME *NIGHT*.

KEVIN KILLED HER. I ORDERED THE POLICE IN FOR YOU.

BUT *YOU*--YOU WOULDN'T BE *CAUGHT*--AND YOU WOULDN'T *STOP*--

--AND NOW KEVIN IS DEAD AND YOU'RE HERE TO KILL ME.

WILL THAT GIVE YOU SATISFACTION, MY SON? KILLING A HELPLESS OLD MAN?

THE KILLING, NO. NO SATISFACTION. BUT EVERYTHING UP UNTIL THE KILLING WILL BE A GAS.

YOU CAN SCREAM NOW IF YOU WANT TO.

IT'S BEAUTIFUL, GOLDIE. IT'S PERFECT. IT'S JUST LIKE I PROMISED ONLY BETTER.

KEVIN WAS DAMN FRUSTRATING BUT ROARK'S A PURE JOY.

IT'S NOT QUICK OR QUIET LIKE IT WAS WITH YOU. NO, IT'S LOUD AND NASTY. MY KIND OF KILL.

I STARE THE BASTARD IN THE FACE AND I LAUGH AS HE SCREAMS TO GOD FOR MERCY AND I LAUGH HARDER WHEN HE SQUEALS LIKE A STUCK PIG AND WHEN HE WHIMPERS LIKE A BABY I'M LAUGHING SO HARD I CRY.

HE SPURTS AND GURGLES AND LIFE IS GOOD.

AND WHEN HIS EYES GO DEAD THE HELL I SEND HIM TO MUST SEEM LIKE HEAVEN AFTER WHAT I'VE DONE TO HIM.

FREEZE!

OH MY GOD...

BREKK

BREKK

BRAKA

JERKS! THEY SHOULD HAVE SHOT ME IN THE HEAD--AND ENOUGH TIMES TO MAKE SURE.

A FEW DAYS LATER I CLAW MY WAY OUT OF A HAZE OF ANESTHETICS. IT'S UP TO THE DOCTORS FOR NOW, THE DOCTORS AND THE REAL HARD WORKERS, THE NURSES.

IT'S STUPID. EVERYBODY KNOWS WHAT'S COMING BUT THEY GO THROUGH THE MOTIONS ANYWAY. WHAT A WASTE OF TIME.

MONTHS FALL OFF THE CALENDAR WHILE I BREATHE AND EAT THROUGH TUBES AND I CAN'T EVEN WASH MYSELF OR USE A TOILET LIKE A GROWN MAN OUGHT TO.

NIGHT AFTER NIGHT I WAIT FOR SOMEBODY TO COME AND FINISH ME OFF. AFTER A WHILE I REALIZE IT'S NOT GOING TO BE SO EASY AS THAT. I'M A MONKEY WRENCH STUCK IN A GREAT BIG MACHINE AND I'VE CAUSED SOME DAMAGE AND IT'LL TAKE A GOOD LONG TIME FOR THE GEARS TO GRIND ME TO POWDER.

I'M ON MY FEET FOR ABOUT TEN MINUTES BEFORE THE COPS KICK THEM OUT FROM UNDER ME. THEY DON'T ASK ME ANY QUESTIONS. THEY JUST KEEP KNOCKING THE CRAP OUT OF ME AND WAVING A CONFESSION IN MY FACE.

AND I KEEP SPITTING BLOOD ALL OVER IT AND LAUGHING AT HOW MANY FRESH COPIES THEY COME UP WITH.

MOSTLY I DON'T FEEL THE PUNISHMENT. I'M OFF, FAR AWAY, WATCHING IT ALL GO PAST LIKE AN OLD MOVIE YOU ALREADY KNOW THE END OF.

THEN ALONG COMES THIS WORMY ASSISTANT DISTRICT ATTORNEY WHO TURNS THE RECORDER OFF AND SAYS IF I DON'T SIGN THEIR CONFESSION THEY'LL KILL MY MOM.

I BREAK HIS ARM IN THREE PLACES AND SIGN THE CONFESSION.

FROM THEN ON IT'S THE CIRCUS EVERYBODY WANTS IT TO BE. THEY NAIL ME FOR THE WORKS, NOT JUST THE PEOPLE I DID KILL BUT EVEN LUCILLE AND THE GIRLS ROARK AND KEVIN ATE.

AND EVEN GOLDIE.

THE JUDGE IS ALL FIRE AND BRIMSTONE WHEN SHE HANDS DOWN THE SENTENCE. THE CROWD EATS IT UP.

AND RIGHT NOW THEY'RE OUTSIDE, WAITING. HOLDING A VIGIL, THEY CALL IT. THEY'RE HOLLERING AND PULLING SIX-PACKS OUT OF THEIR STATION WAGONS AND WISHING THEY COULD WATCH THE LYNCHING UP CLOSE. THEY'LL HAVE TO SETTLE FOR WATCHING THE LIGHTS DIM.

MIDNIGHT AND MY DEATH ARE ONLY A FEW HOURS AWAY WHEN I GET MY FIRST SURPRISE IN EIGHTEEN MONTHS.

MY ONLY VISITOR.

THEY'VE GOT ME IN A CELL ABOUT A MILE AWAY FROM THE OTHER CONS SO I CAN HEAR HER HEELS CLICK ON THE CEMENT FLOOR FOR A LONG TIME BEFORE SHE GETS HERE.

I'M READY FOR ANYTHING BUT THAT SCENT.

I GOT THEM FOR YOU GOOD, DIDN'T I, GOLDIE?

195

THEY FIX ME A
PRETTY DECENT
STEAK FOR MY
LAST MEAL. THEY
EVEN THROW IN A
BREW, THE FIRST
I'VE HAD SINCE
BACK AT NANCY'S.

THEN THEY
SHAVE MY HEAD
AND FIX ME WITH
A RUBBER DIAPER
AND GET TO IT.

AND IT'S ABOUT
DAMN TIME, IF
YOU ASK ME.

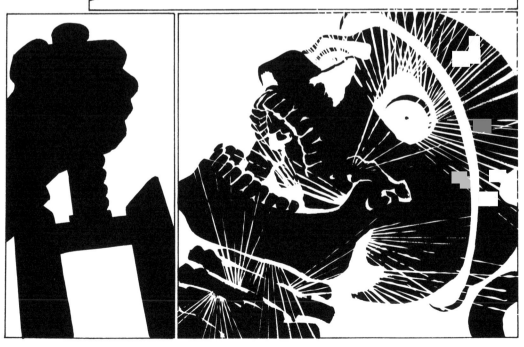

THE
END

THIS ONE RAN AWAY WITH ITSELF. I'd planned it as forty-eight pages, but I got carried away. It's all Marv's fault. The big lug started bossing me around. It's like that sometimes. The pages you're looking at right now feature some of the covers and publicity pieces I drew in the course of *Sin City*'s thirteen-month run in *Dark Horse Presents*.

— FM

FM '91